How to Analyze

People

The Complete Guide to Read People Instantly. Analyze Body Language and Human Behaviours. Manipulate and Persuade though Dark Psychology

By Victor Murphy

Legal Disclaimer

The information contained in this book and its contents is not designed to replace any form of medical or professional advice; and is not meant to replace the need for independent medical, financial, legal, or other professional advice or services that may be required. The content and information in this book have been provided for educational and entertainment purposes only.

The content and information contained in this book have been compiled from sources deemed reliable, and they are accurate to the best of the Author's knowledge, information, and belief. However, the Author cannot guarantee its accuracy and validity and therefore cannot be held liable for any errors and/or omissions. Further, changes are periodically made to this book as needed. Where appropriate and/or necessary, you must consult a professional (including but not limited to your doctor, attorney, financial advisor, or other such professional) before using any of the suggested remedies, techniques, and/or information in this book.

Upon using this book's contents and information, you agree to hold harmless the Author from any damages, costs, and expenses, including any legal fees, potentially resulting from the application of any of the information in this book. This disclaimer applies to any loss, damages, or injury caused by the use and application of this book's contents, whether direct-

Table of Contents

Introduction

Can you read people well? Are you able to look at someone and tell from the way they are standing, the behavior their emitting, and the words they choose, what their real intentions are, or how they are feeling?

Some people are born with a gift which enables them to have a certain sixth sense about such things, whilst others need to work at developing this in a manual way. This is your intuition, your inner voice, and understanding it and trusting it will help you to read those around you like a very good book!

There are many situations in life when it is beneficial to be able to read between the lines a little and understand what someone is really intending, especially in this day and age. Unfortunately, not everyone has pure intentions at heart, and there are some unscrupulous people around. Being able to read and analyze people means that you can quickly identify what someone true intentions are, thus sidestepping any potential issues in the future.

Whilst it's not always the case that first impressions are right, by understanding what to look for, analyzing the information you have to hand, and learning to listen to and trust your intuition, you'll find it far easier to develop strong and accurate impressions of other people and their actions/intentions.

This book is designed to help you learn the art of analyzing others. We're going to talk about the power of words and how to use them correctly, including what to look for when someone is saying one thing, but clearly means another. We're also going to talk about non-verbal cues, i.e. body language. It's often the case that words being spoken and body language do not agree with one another at all - this is a huge red flag. In this case, trust the body language, because it cannot and does not lie!

We're also going to talk about ways to develop your intuition, and when used in conjunction with the other advice and tools in the book, you'll become a pro at analyzing others before you know it! Before we get to that point however, we need to discuss why the ability to effectively and accurately analyze others is important, and the situations it may be useful in. We're going to cover that in our first chapter, introducing you in more detail to the whole subject, and moving forward from there in a practical and relatable way.

So, without further ado, let's get started!

Chapter 1
Why Analyzing Others Will
Help You in Your Life

Analyzing other people isn't meant to be negative in your life, and we're certainly not encouraging you to become suspicious of everyone you meet. The fact remains that being able to read other people will allow you to realize when you're being lied to and manipulated, and these are always situations to avoid wherever possible.

Most of us like to believe the best in people, and we're always looking for the good, trying to avoid the bad. Wouldn't it be easier if we could read the intentions of someone else, and not put ourselves through the long-winded drama and trauma of being lied to or manipulated? Being able to effectively analyze other people, whilst also being able to give them the benefit of the doubt in certain situations, is key.

Is analyzing other people always 100% accurate? Not always, but most of the time you'll be right. First impressions are so very important these days, but we do need to bear in mind that certain elements can cloud the way someone is acting. For instance, a shy person may come over as quite rude or antisocial, when in actual fact they are feeling awkward and unsure of themselves. Being able to read nonverbal clues, such as body language, and being able to analyze the things they say and how they say them, will allow you to realize this is shyness and not a basically rude person you're dealing with. From that, you might be able to form a friendship with this person, helping them to overcome the shyness which may have troubled them so far in their life.

There are countless situations where being able to analyze and read other people is useful, and it will enhance your life and the relationships you have with people as a result.

Situations When Analyzing Others is of Benefit

In our introduction to this chapter, we have already highlighted one particular situation when reading people closely might be a beneficial thing, e.g. in the event of a shy person who is struggling to deal with a social situation. There are countless others, however.

For instance, isn't it better to know if someone is lying to you? Isn't it better to know if someone is attempting to do something underhanded? Being able to carefully analyze someone's words and actions, whilst reading the silent language of their posture and body language will allow you to understand that something is a little 'off'. From there you can work to explore what this is, and perhaps let this person know that you are on to them and that they had better come clean!

Body language experts have made a fortune out of being able to read non-verbal cues, as well as analyze the words that are spoken. A lot of the time, words and actions don't add up, they simply won't work for hand in hand, and from there you can tell that something else is going on under the surface. Reading between the lines will allow you to understand what is really going on, without really having to dig too much and perhaps accuse someone of something they aren't guilty of.

There are many situations in which reading between the lines is beneficial, but perhaps no more so than in a personal situation. Whilst we're not going to suggest you read your partner's body language and try to work out wheth-er they're cheating on you or not, the fact re-mains that if this is happening to you, if you suspect something might be going on, being able to analyze your partner's behavior and their body language will give you more clues as to what the truth it. This might, unfortunately, lead you to a confession, and from there you can make your next move. It might also lead you to valise that your suspicions were wrong, and you have avoided accusing your loved one of something they just haven't done.

Of course, on a more positive note, being able to analyze a friend might help you to under-stand that something is wrong. Not everyone likes to open up and talk about their worries and fears, but their body language will clearly tell you that something is wrong. If you're not sure what to look for, you might simply let it go, shrug it off perhaps. On the other hand, if you know what to look for, and combined with the fact that you know this person on a deeper level, you'll be able to spot the telltale signs and simply let your friend know that you're there for them. This might be enough for them to open up and let you help them solve their problem.

As you can see, analyzing people can help in many different situations, from understanding different personalities at work, to help you in your personal life.

How the Police and CIA Analyze People in a Criminal Situation

Most police officers are well drilled in reading body language. Why? Because if a criminal is trying to get away with a crime, they're hardly likely to come right out and admit it! In this case, reading their body language, picking apart the word they say and questioning them in a specific kind of way can often enough to either pull a confession out of them or make them trip themselves up enough to open extra questioning.

If you think about how people behave when they are guilty of something or they're scared/worried, it's totally different to how they behave when nothing is going on, when they're totally innocent and free of any guilt. The signs of guilt include:

- Fidgeting, especially with the hands and feet
- Not making eye contact
- Stumbling over their words, perhaps stammering or laughing/stalling for time when answering questions
- Refusing to answer questions at all
- Crossing their arms over their body or their legs over each other - this is a classic barrier type of body language, a defensive stance
- Sweating

- Flushing of the facial skin
- Shaking

When someone is showing these signs, either all or just some, it paints a clear picture that there is something that isn't being vocally communicated. Most people will crack under pressure, so experts know that if they see these signs, to push a little harder. If someone is truly innocent, they're not going to crack and admit something they haven't done; on the other hand, if someone is hiding guilt, enough of a push may just get them to confess.

As you can see, in this case, the ability to analyze what someone isn't saying, but what their body is screaming, is extremely effective. You don't have to be a member of the police force or CIA to use these techniques, and they are equally as effective in everyday life.

Being Aware of How You Are Analyzed by Others

Before we move and begin to look towards practical elements of the book, we should point out that whilst you're analyzing other people, there is a fair chance that someone is also analyzing you! This isn't meant to make you paranoid, but it helps to realize this because it can allow you to understand body language and how the mind automatically reacts to certain situations.

Do you believe you can control your own body language? In certain conscious situations, yes you can. For instance, in a job interview, you know you're going to be nervous, so you can consciously work to calm yourself down and help to reduce the negative body language signs you might be exhibiting. This includes knowing not to cross your arms or legs over your body, taking deep breaths to calm any nerves, and making an effort to hold eye contact and smile with the interviewing panel.

On the other hand, if you're caught in the middle of a lie, do you think you could be 'at the moment' enough to keep up with the verbal side of the lie, think on your feet, and control your body language at the same time? No! If you were a professional liar, maybe you could to a certain degree, but body language will give you away time and time again if the other person knows what to look for.

Key Points From This Chapter

We've introduced you to the whole idea of analyzing someone in this chapter and you now know why it is an important skill to develop. The key points you need to remember from this chapter, moving forward are:

- Body language is something which cannot be controlled in most situations, however, when you know a situation is about to occur, you can control it to a degree
- The police often use body language skills to be able to analyze whether someone is telling the truth or not, in conjunction with careful questioning
- As you analyze people, remember that they may be analyzing you
- The ability to analyze another person is key in helping you to avoid difficult situations in life, or helping you to understand the difference between the truth and a lie
- Your intuition is something which will help to guide you, but you need to learn to trust it first

Chapter 2

The Unspoken Word

We've hinted a lot towards body language in our first chapter, but this chapter is going to delve a little deeper and talk about the power of body language, what to look out for, how to interpret it, and how to tie it together in terms of the situation you're in.

First things first, what is body language?

Body language is what your body does without being consciously told to by your brain. Body language is completely subconscious. You don't tell your brain to make you sweat when you're nervous, it's a completely unconscious action which is linked to this particular emotion. Your brain senses the emotion and it kicks in the 'fight or flight' response. This was born from the days of the cavemen and women, and it's something we haven't yet grown out of!

During these times, our ancestors were at risk of all manner of large and big-toothed predators, and this 'fight or flight' or response kept them safe, helping them to always be on guard for threats to their survival. Of course, when your brain perceives a threat these days, it's hardly likely to be anything of the saber-toothed tiger type, but it still senses danger and kicks your survival mechanisms into action. This is why you sweat, shake, can't get your words out, fidget, etc. These non-verbal cues are a great way to understand how someone is feeling without them actually having to form words and tell you.

As we mentioned in our last chapter, body language cannot be controlled when it is linked to a subconscious reaction, and it can only be reined in when dealing with a situation that you know is going to cause a certain emotion. We mentioned the job interview situation, but you could also say perhaps going on a first date, or any other situation which is going to kick your 'fight or flight' response into action. By knowing about this beforehand, you can be more aware of how your body is behaving, and you can tone it down. You can't stop it completely, but you can limit the effects and perhaps disguise them.

Of course, you might be reading this and wondering why there are professional con artists walking the Earth. If reading body language was so easy, surely they would have been rumbled by now? Well, not necessarily. There are body language experts who can read body language and pick up cues, but there are always people who have learned to understand their own body language and limit it in every situation. These are the most dangerous of people because they know how their body reacts when they lie, and they have perfected the art of controlling their body language. This isn't a subconscious reaction in this case, because they know they're going to be questioned, it's something they have pre-empted and rehearsed.

Despite that, there is always something that will trip them up, but you have to look very closely in order to spot it!

The Power of Body Language

Body language is extremely powerful because it can completely change the meaning of your words. For instance, if someone is speaking and attempting to sound cheerful and happy, but their body language is dour and miserable, what are you going to believe? Of course, you'll believe their general demeanor. You can't say "oh I'm so happy, I woke up with such a smile on my face this morning" but accompany it with a frown, lowered eyes, and hunched shoulders. It simply doesn't wash. You could also listen to the tone of their voice, and it could be as up-beat as anything, but their body language would make you question it all.

A little earlier we mentioned that being able to read between the lines and analyze another person is important because it can help you spot situations in which friends might be strug-gling but not telling you. This is where body language would do the talking. Your friend could be saying all the right things, but if they refuse to meet your eyes, their general posture is slumped and they're not smiling, constantly fidgeting, and looking irritated, you're not going to take what they're saying at face value, and rightly so.

Learning to read body language will take time, and at first, you might question what you're seeing and wonder if what you're thinking is correct. A little later in the book, we're going to talk about intuition and how to start to trust your inner voice and let it guide you in your decisions. The more you can do this, the abler you will be to read body language effectively, without questioning yourself in the process.

A person who wants to trick and manipulate will move towards a person who doesn't trust their own gut, and someone who isn't that au fait with the art of reading body language. They aren't going to spend much time around a person who can read them like a book! Handily, this is something you can learn.

Non-Verbal Cues to Look Out For

So, what do you need to look for when it comes to reading body language?

Different signs will lead you toward different conclusions. Before we get onto what body language might mean, let's look at some of the most common non-verbal cues to be on the lookout for. When you see these signs, usually within a combination, you can read between the lines and come to a conclusion, which throws their words out of context.

Common body language signs include:

- Avoiding eye contact
- Holding eye contact deliberately for too long, e.g. not blinking
- Eyes flitting around, e.g. looking everywhere but at you, blinking a lot
- Fast or shallow breathing
- Flushed skin on the face
- Sweating

- Fidgeting, especially hands or feet. This could be wringing the hands or tapping the foot
- Crossing the arms over the body - a defensive stance
- Sitting with one leg crossed over the other, or standing in the same way - again, a defensive move
- Biting the lip

In order to get a very clear picture of what is going on, it's important to read body language alongside the words being said, as well as how they are said, e.g. tone of voice, how fast they are speaking, etc. We will get onto the verbalized side of analysis shortly, but for now, body language is our focus.

When you notice these key body language signs, that person's body is basically speaking for them. We mentioned earlier that sometimes you can control your body language if you're conscious of the situation beforehand, e.g.a date or a job interview. Usually, however, when a situation is placed unexpectedly upon a person, their body language cannot be controlled because they haven't had the time to prepare. They will also give themselves away by tumbling over their words.

To help you see how this body language can help you shape a conclusion, let's look at a few common situations you might find yourself in, and how you can read body language at that time.

Situation 1 - Someone is upset about something, but not telling you

Perhaps a friend seems a little 'off', but you can't quite put your finger on why. They are saying all the right things, e.g. "I'm fine", "I'm just a little tired", but you're not buying it. How might their body language tell you that your suspicions are right?

In this case, their body language might be similar to someone who is lying, but not in a negative way. Look for signs such as:

- Slumped shoulders
- A distracted vibe, e.g. you have to repeat yourself a few times, they seem 'off with the fairies'
- Refusing to make eye contact for longer than a second
- Crossing their arms over their body
- Staring into space for much of the time

These are classic signs to look for in someone who has something on their mind, but they're just not sharing it with you. By reading this body language and using it in conjunction with the knowledge you have about the person, you can come to a conclusion and try and encourage them to talk. Of course, everyone is different, but if you know this person well, you'll probably get an inkling that something isn't quite right. By reading their body language you'll be able to gain more information on whether your suspicions are right, or whether they are misplaced.

Situation 2 - Someone is lying and have been caught out

The biggest advantage of being able to analyze people is that you can understand when someone is lying to you. Unless you know what to look for and you can read the signs, you're open to being manipulated, but once you have these analysis skills within your armory, you'll easily be able to know the score without having to tie yourself up in knots wondering whether you're being paranoid or not.

Someone who is lying is unable to hide their body language unless they are a very good liar. In this case, you would need to use more information than just their body language, e.g. background information, so-called facts that don't add up, the words they're saying, etc. Even a very good liar will trip themselves up somehow, but their body language is something you can watch very closely to give you extra information.

Someone who is lying to you, and about to get caught out will usually show the following body language signs:

- Refuses point blank to make eye contact, and if they do, it will be very fleeting
- Breathing a little faster than normal
- They may blink more often than normal, and look around the room - anywhere but at you

- They will cross their arms over their body in defense
- Sweating
- Flushed skin
- Fidgeting, especially tapping a foot or wringing the fingers

There will be verbal cues too, but in terms of the body language they exhibit, these are the main ones to look out for.

Situation 3 - Someone is angry about something

You probably won't need to be able to read too much to see that someone is angry, but there are people who hide their anger well, and then it erupts. Learning what to look for in simple situations is key in building up your foundations of analyzing people well. In this case, anger is a very useful case study to look at.

Someone who is angry cannot control their body language at all. Once they near the point of total explosion, they have literally zero control over anything and it's useful to be able to read their body language before they reach that point so that you can either move away from the situation or do your best to try and diffuse it if you are able.

The main body language signs that someone is building with anger are:

- Strong breathing - faster, stronger, and you will be able to hear it
- Flushed skin, usually quite red
- No problems in holding eye contact, in fact, they will hold it for a long time without blinking
- Clenched fists
- Sweating

Can you see the difference in body language in someone who is trying to hide something, versus someone who isn't? Someone who is lying is trying to manipulate you into not learning about something, trying to deceive you. Someone who is trying not to let on that they are upset about something is almost doing the same, but not in a negative way, almost in a well-meaning way. With a few minor exceptions, the body language shown in these two situations is quite similar. However, the body language in the anger scenario, i.e. someone who isn't hiding anything, someone who is quite open about how they're feeling, is very different.

It's interesting to be able to compare and contrast. Someone who isn't hiding something will hold your eye contact, almost in defiance, someone who is, will not. That's the basic rule to look out for.

Common Patterns of Analyzing Others

Aside from body language, what else should you look out for when analyzing other people? What patterns do you need to put together to bring you to a solid conclusion?

Words can mean nothing if their body language is screaming something different. Similarly, body language might be conflicted, and that could throw you off course.

The best way to analyze someone is to check their body language, the words they are saying, how they are saying them, e.g. their tone of voice, the speed at which they're talking, and whether they stumble over their words or not, as well as taking into account the situation itself.

You might think this is a time-consuming process, and one which isn't going to allow you to analyze anyone very quickly, but it will get far quicker the more you do it. If you think about when you learn to drive a car; at first you think you cannot imagine ever being able to do these things without really paying much conscious attention to what your hand is doing and when, but you learn to do it almost without thinking. It's the same with analyzing people, and the more you do it, the more you practice, the more it will become second nature. When your intuition starts to flare up and tell you something isn't right, you'll know when to pay attention, and you'll be able to use that inner voice as a guide, along with the tools we're teaching you in this book.

Key Points From This Chapter

Learning to read body language will help you in so many different areas of your life, not just in the art of analyzing people in general. The words that someone says are often far from the mark of truth, but unless someone is very good at lying, they're unlikely to be able to stop everybody language sign from appearing.

The main takeaway points from this chapter are:

- Body language is a mostly subconscious technique used by the brain when it senses a threat/to ensure the survival
- The common body language signs are often totally in conflict with the words that the person is telling you
- Different signs lend themselves to different situations
- A person who is trying to deceive you will often refuse to meet your eye
- Learning to read body language can help to give you an insight into the truth behind a person's words, and this can help you to either move away from a situation, or help

someone who may not want to admit they're struggling

- Learning to trust your body language reading skills will take time, but will also get easier the more you do it

Chapter 3

How to Interpret Words

Our last chapter was all about the things that someone isn't saying, but how do you interpret the things they are saying? Are they always lying? Are they always trying to hide something? Not always!

It's important to first take words at face value and only delve deeper into the situation if you really feel that what they're saying to you isn't exactly accurate. Again, this is something which your intuition will help you with. You cannot go around doubting everything that people say to you - firstly, you'll just end up paranoid, and secondly, you will be exhausted from reading too much into every single thing!

Analyzing people isn't about becoming untrusting and doubting every single word, it's about knowing the situations which may cause a little doubt to come your way and using the techniques to delve a little deeper into the truth of the situation. You shouldn't become deeply suspicious simply because someone says something to you which at first doesn't seem to add up - there could be a very good explanation for it.

For instance, if your partner tells you that they're working latest the office. Believe them. The very basis of a relationship is about trust. The only situation in which you should start to analyze your partner a little is when several late nights occur, and other things simply don't fit the pattern. Only analyze when your gut tells you to do so, and not simply because something is out of routine. By reading too much into everything you risk driving yourself crazy, but you also risk ruining relationships for nothing more than unfounded distrust.

The point of this is that you should listen to words and take them at face value unless you have reason to believe otherwise.

Reading Between The Lines

If you really do feel that the words that are being spoken aren't really the truth of the situation, what can you look for verbally? We've already spoken at length about body language, and you should certainly use what you've learned on that subject in conjunction with the words you're hearing. If someone is lying to you then their body language and their verbal words will be totally at odds. In that case, believe the body language because it rarely lies.

You've surely heard the old saying 'actions speak louder than words', and that is very firm truth. When we're caught in the middle of a situation which we want to get out of, we tend to try and talk our way out of it first of all. We'll try and explain, but our words might get tangled up and we might stumble. Whilst we're doing this, our body is kick-starting that 'fight or flight' response we mentioned earlier. This is when the sweating starts, the flushed skin, the fidgeting. As the explanation doesn't seem to work, we're likely to get frustrated with ourselves because our words aren't working and we can't get them out eloquently. Then we become stressed at ourselves, and we might sweat a little more, mop our brow, fidget more, undo the top button of a shirt, etc.

If you were watching this situation you would instantly have your lights on alert and realize that something wasn't quite right.

The situation moves on as words become higher in pitch, the speed of conversation gets faster, and you're desperately trying to get the other person to see your side of things believe your lie, but you know deep down it's not working. You will not hold their eye because you know they know that you're not telling them the truth, and you feel guilty.

The overall situation is clear when you combine the body language signs with the way verbal cues work. Can you see how easy it can be once you know what to look for?

Surely, you've been caught in a situation before when you maybe lied or bent the truth a little, and you tried desperately to get out of it? Come on, admit it, we're all human after all! How did you feel? Try and think back to a time like that and imagine how your body language and your words combined together. Understanding how you respond to certain situations yourself can help you read other people to a certain degree.

The bottom line is that the truth of a tricky situation is usually found somewhere between the lines, i.e. somewhere between the words coming out of the person's mouth and the actions they're showing you visually.

Choice of Words Versus Tone

The words a person chooses to use can say a lot about what is really going on beneath the surface. When you analyze this with the way they say them, and what their body is saying at the same time, you can gather enough information to really get to the heart of the matter.

There are two things to look out for in terms of the choice of words. Firstly, they may opt for long words, e.g. try to blind you with science, and therefore choose words that they think you might not know the meaning of. The hope, in this case, is that you will simply nod along and let the matter drop. On the other hand, they may stumble over their words and use a quite simple language, because their brain is going too fast to try and be coherent.

What does all that mean?

You can't tell from their choice of words alone; you need the rest of the information to hand to be able to get a full picture. For instance, it's quite possible that someone is lying to you if they're using simple words, with many 'erm', 'ah', er' thrown in. This means you've caught them off guard. It could however also mean that you've touched upon a subject that they're just not comfortable with, and from that, you would need to read their body language to really get to the bottom of what the issue is.

Someone who is using overly complicated language could be lying and using these words to try and throw you off the scent. In this case, you're probably dealing with a very professional liar! It could also be that someone is quite nervous and is trying their best to impress, but whether or not they make sense depends on the subject they're talking about and how they articulate themselves under pressure.

Again, it's impossible to analyze someone solely by the words they choose, but it is an element in putting the puzzle together and coming to a decision.

Speed And Tone

The other thing to look out for, aside from the words they use and how they say them (tone), is how it all links into the speed they're talking. If someone is talking fast, they are either lying, scared, nervous, angry, or upset. If someone is talking slow, they could be not at all bothered about what you're saying, completely disinterested, or distracted by something else.

The speed at which someone is talking can be interpreted with the tone, e.g. the way it is being said. There are several ways to say something. For instance, saying something with a slight inflection in your voice at the end, raising the tone slightly could mean that you're turning a statement into a question. However, keeping your voice flat means it is a statement and not a question. In many different situations, whether you're asking a question or stating something can be a huge game changer.

You could also talk about sarcasm within this subject. Whilst sarcasm is sometimes used as humor, it is also sometimes used to throw you off the scent, make you question what you were saying (question yourself), or it can be a sign of arrogance. Again, you can't tell from the tone alone, and you need to take in the rest of the story in order to get the full picture.

If someone is talking quite fast, their body language is showing you signs of irritation or distress, such as sweating, fidgeting, a defensive stance, and they're stumbling over their words a little, that's a good indicator to suggest the person has been caught in a lie, or they're about to be found out in terms of doing something they would rather have kept a secret.

On the other hand, if someone is talking quite slowly, they seem distant, they're using 'erm', 'um', 'ah', a lot, and their body language suggests they're not in the moment, e.g. fidgeting, looking away, sighing, then that could be a sign that there is something wrong and they're very distracted with a problem of some kind.

Knowing what to look for and being able to piece together the signs will give you the information you need to analyze the person and the situation accurately.

Signs to Look Out For

Other than words and body language, are there any other aspects you should be analyzed in order to fully assess the situation and picture? Yes. There are certain behaviors that people adopt when they're feeling a certain way or trying to hide something. For instance, have you ever come across a liar who turns everything around on you? You ask them a question and they turn it rhetorical, doing a full 360 and basically asking you the same thing?

A key example here is a rather upsetting one; someone who has found out their partner has been cheating. When confronting the cheating partner, it's possible that they will deny it, but there are many signs to look out for which will tell you whether or not to listen to their denial. The first thing a cheater will do when faced with their behavior is to reflect what they've been doing back at you. In this case, you will probably be accused of cheating on them; they will come up with some very random event from the past which they have somehow gleamed cheating from. It will make nose sense, it will be infuriating, but it is designed to make you stop and think for a second, and then hopefully give you enough time to decide you've got it all wrong. In this case, the cheater gets away with it and can breathe easily.

There are several types of behavior which fit into this category, and it really depends on the situation and the person, along with their body language and verbal language, which will show you the whole situation. A few behaviors to be on the lookout for include:

- Turning things around on you
- Blaming you for the thing you're accusing them of/suggesting they have done
- Accusing you of the same thing you're accusing them of/suggesting they have done
- Becoming angry very fast
- Trying to distract you away from the conversation/suggestion
- Using your hot spots or pressing your buttons to try and distract you into anger or confrontation. By doing this, they can twist things and "win" the argument
- Trying to win your sympathy by recalling a sad situation or issue

These types of behavior can be used by anyone, but they are all common narcissistic behavior patterns too. Gaslighting may also come into the equation here, i.e. turning things around onto another person and making the question and doubt themselves. In this case, the narcissistic hopes that the other person drops the conversation and lets them be. In severe cases, a narcissist can make someone doubt their own sanity with a slow and steady approach to gas lighting.

You've no doubt heard of gas lighting in the past, as it is a point which is very much in the news these days. More and more people are waking up to the damaging effects of associating with a narcissistic person and just how terrible gaslighting can be over a period of time.

Of course, the type of behavior a person exhibits may not be as severe as gas lighting, but it is still a distraction technique to try and throw you off the scent. For instance, someone who quickly gets angry and starts talking about things which have no relevance to the subject you've mentioned is clearly trying to take the heat away from the situation and hope that you move on and drop it. The idea here is that you won't want to provoke them any further, so you don't bring the subject up again.

Being on the lookout for these types of distraction techniques and behavior elements will help to continue your journey and your insight into analyzing people more clearly.

Key Points From This Chapter

In this chapter, we have talked about the verbal clues to look for when trying to analyze a person. We have covered language/words chosen, tone, speed, and other types of behavior which go hand in hand with the verbal side of the subject. Of course, you have to use all of this information in alignment with body language too, in order to create a full picture of what to look for.

The main points to take away from this chapter are:

- The choice of words someone uses is key - look for simple words and many 'ah', 'um', 'erm', or overly complicated words
- The tone is important in understanding someone's true intentions
- The speed at which someone speaks is key
- Distraction techniques, such as gas lighting, becoming angry, turning things around on you, are all ways to try and throw someone off the scent of a lie or something being found out
- Analyzing a narcissist can be difficult, because they are masters of deception, often using gaslighting techniques to push a person into doubting their ideas or their own sanity

Chapter 4

Real Intentions or a Clever Mask?

The problem when you first begin to try and analyze people deeply is that you can easily get it wrong. In our next chapter, we're going to talk about intuition and why it is important to listen to your gut a little, as well as taking into account all the information you have already discovered.

People aren't always trying to fool you, either intentionally or unintentionally, and sometimes they may just be having a bad day, not feeling great, or a little distracted about a personal issue. It's very important that you don't take the art of analyzing someone to extremes, otherwise, you may find that your social circle begins to shrink quite quickly!

In this chapter, we're going to explore the fact that in this day and age, many people are wearing a mask, but that an equal number of people are also being genuine. The art of finding out which is in practice and also in keeping an open mind.

How Negative Intentions Can be Masked

A person who is very good at fooling others can often mask their negative intentions by playing the part of a charmer or someone who is the victim. These are both very clever ways to mask intentions and much of the time they actually work. However, as you become more adept at analyzing people, you'll be able to work out whether someone is masking something or not. Of course, masking could be masking a sad situation that they don't want to talk about with someone, or it could be masking an intention to lie or cheat.

Hiding something doesn't always mean negative intentions are there, it can simply mean that a person just doesn't want to talk about it. Figuring out which side of the line the whole situation is on can be difficult at first.

The victim and charmer routines are very popular. Let's explore why.

A person who is charming is someone who everyone likes. Everyone wants to be around that person, they want to be noticed by them, and when they decide to spend time with you, you feel good. They are so witty, wonderful at conversation, and usually quite suave and attractive, that nobody would ever assume them to be up to something negative underneath it all. Of course, it is an act, because this charming person (in this case - not all charming people are hiding something) is deceiving everyone into a sense of invincibility.

If there is a whisper of something negative about this person, everyone brushes it off, assuming that the person raising the concern is just jealous. As you can see, becoming a charmer is quite the bulletproof vest in many ways, and for that reason, throughout history, many criminals, cheaters, and classic deceivers have always been described as "charming".

On the other hand, the victim card is a good one to play too, with equally as much success. We all want to root for the underdog, and we want the person who is having a tough time in life to do well. By playing the victim, someone is trying to glean your sympathy. They are attempting to gain your trust, an emotional connective, and your empathy, and from that, you will never believe that they are up to something negative. They won't only do this with you, they will do it with several other people too.

The problem with the victim game is that it can often backfire. People are only prepared to watch someone play the martyr and be negative in their personality for so long before they become tired and want a dose of positivity instead. From this, you can assume that the charmer routine works more than the victim routine does. Despite that, it's still a situation that many people use, and quite successfully too.

The art of hiding negative intentions is usually done by gaining trust and then deceiving the trusting person they've befriended. When the fallout occurs, and eventually it does, the person who was deceived is often left quite shaking and has problems trusting others in the future. It's hardly surprising, but this is such a common trick by deceivers and manipulators, that it pays to be subtle on the lookout for it, provided you have slight back up evidence to suggest that this may be the case.

Remember, some people are just naturally charming, it doesn't mean they're hiding something; some people are victims in life, and that also doesn't mean they have other intentions. The fact that unscrupulous people use these tactics is unfair to those who are true to themselves and make analyzing others quite difficult, especially for a beginner.

Reading Nerves And Lies

Two of the most common situations you will analyze are when someone is telling a lie, and when someone is crippled with nerves. Both situations are hugely beneficial to learn about because they help you either sidestep a potential manipulation or helps you to understand the other person and help them overcome their nerves in a particular situation.

Reading nerves and lies are distinctly different. Let's look into each one.

When analyzing someone who you assume to be lying, you'll be able to pick up on some key signs pretty quickly.

- **Body language of a liar** - Avoiding eye contact, fidgeting, seeming distracted, arms crossed over the body, or legs crossed if sitting, tapping foot, flushed skin, dilated pupils (if you can see that closely), and perhaps sweating. Of course, this is assuming this person isn't a professional liar; in that case, they will probably hold your gaze and try and stare you out. This is something else to be on the lookout for.
- **Verbal cues of a liar** - Contradicting themselves, using 'erm' to bide their time on what to say next, possibly using long words to try

and bamboozle you, speaking fast, sarcasm, questioning tone.

- **Behavior traits of a liar** - Being irritated when you question what they are saying, may try and turn the situation around on you, distraction techniques, and outright denial.

In comparison, let's look at how someone might behave if they're nervous.

- **Body language of someone who is nervous** - Fidgeting, pulling at the neck of their clothes and the cuffs, tapping their foot, sweating, flushed skin, fast and audible breathing, seeming distracted/away with the fairies. May hold your gaze in a 'help me' manner.
- **Verbal cues of someone who is nervous** - Speaking fast or extremely slow, using a lot of 'erm', 'um', 'ah', and not being able to find

the right words. Usually uses quite short words and stumbles over them.

- **Behavior traits of someone who is nervous** - Not seeming to be present at the moment and can be quite frustrating to speak to. Usually asks a lot of 'what if' questions which may or may not have anything to do with the problem or situation at hand. They are doing this to try and make themselves feel better, i.e. the situation isn't as bad as it seems.

As you can see, one situation is a negative intention, and the other one is someone who is just dealing with negative emotion. As you become more experienced and au fait with analyzing people, you'll be able to spot both classic situations very easily. Someone who is lying may be quite convincing, but there will always be something in their body language which gives them away. Someone who is nervous will literally be obviously nervous. They won't try and trick you and they won't try and get away from the conversation - they are so consumed by their nerves that they can't think of anything else.

The Importance of Keeping an Open Mind

We have touched upon this already, but it is vitally important that we emphasize it once more - not everyone has negative intentions at heart. The idea of analyzing people isn't always about spotting cheaters and liars, although that is certainly a beneficial part of it. Analyzing people is about being able to spot emotional barriers, and possibly being able to use your natural empathy to help that person open up.

As humans, we tend to focus so much on the negative that it's hard to see anything else, and we tend to try and bulletproof our lives so that nothing bad happens to us. The problem is, life is about positive and negatives, and it's impossible to try and spot every negative thing before it happens. You simply have to roll with the punches.

The point of being able to analyze others is to be aware and to be able to help or sidestep a situation if it presents itself to you. It's not for you to go around accusing everyone of lying or hiding something; every single day we all tell small white lies, and most of these aren't damaging at all. Our body language will give us away if someone deems it suitable to look hard enough, but you need to work out for yourself which situations are worth your time and focus, and which aren't. It's far better to focus your attention on helping other people in situations than trying to blame others for things they might not have done.

For instance, if you see a friend and you suspect there is something wrong with them, analyze their behavior and their words and try and figure it out. From that you can help them open up, encouraging them to talk. You have no idea how helpful this might be to them.

For that reason, using your people analyzing skills for good is far better than suddenly becoming the unofficial cheating and lying police!

Key Points From This Chapter

Learning to analyze people takes time and effort, but it can turn out to be a very useful tool to have in your armory. However, that doesn't mean that you need to analyze every single person or situation you come into contact with!

When you first begin on your analyzing journey, you'll no doubt be tempted to read too much into everything, but it's important to remember balance. Some people just have a bad day, or maybe they're going through something in their private lives. This can cause a normally very even-keeled person to act a little out of character and it's not something you should take too much to heart or become suspicious about. The art of analyzing people is about using the skill when it is required, rather than on a constant basis.

The main points to take away from this chapter are:

- It can be easy for someone to mask negative intentions, and try and fool you into believing a lie
- Understanding the difference between someone who is lying and someone who is simply nervous is key
- A nervous person isn't trying to trick you and isn't trying to deceive you, they are simply

caught up in their own moment and their own heads, and are completely distracted by whatever situation is going on

- It is important to keep an open mind and realize that people may simply be going through something personal, as an explanation for their behavior. This doesn't mean that you need to analyze them too closely
- Learning how to analyze people is best used for situations which you are either very concerned about in terms of someone, or yourself, being deceived, or in situations which could help another person, e.g. a friend upset about something and not opening up to you.

Chapter 5

How to Develop Personal Perception and Intuition

One of the biggest tools you have at your disposal is already within you, but you probably don't listen to it or trust it.

Every single day we experience hunches or gut feelings, but most of us don't pay much attention to them. The thing is, those hunches are the key to unlocking your analysis potential. Those hunches are there to keep you safe, to help you understand other people, and to allow you to make better, more reliable decisions overall.

You have no doubt heard the term 'mother's intuition'. The truth is that you don't have to be a mother to have intuition - everyone has it!

The term itself comes from the survival mechanism of a mother trying to keep her child safe. It is the innate ability to simply know something without actually having a reason to know it. It's probably happened to you before; maybe you just had a strange feeling that something was going on with someone, and you tried to add logic and reason to it, telling yourself that there was nothing going on, everything was fine, but you later found out that they had been going through a hard time.

In that situation, if you had listened to your gut, the hunch you had been experiencing, you could have possibly spoken to the person a little more deeply, not taken "I'm fine" at face value.

In some extreme cases, intuition can even keep you alive. People have reported gut feelings telling them not to do something, e.g. don't drive down that street, it looks too dark. That person ignored that hunch and drove down that street anyway because they saw no logical reason not to. The car crashed.

It's not something mystical and otherworldly, it's simply your subconscious mind trying to give you clues and guide you in the right direction. The thing is, when you start to trust and listen to your intuition, it can become a very useful tool in daily life.

Your intuition can:

• Help you make better decisions
• Help you weight up logic versus emotional reasoning and come to a suitable middle ground
• Help to keep you safe
• Help you understand a situation better

- Help you understand if someone is hiding something or is upset about something
- Give you the missing piece to a metaphorical jigsaw
- Help you to analyze people and situations

One of the biggest parts of being able to analyze people isn't only about knowing what to look for and piecing everything together, it's also about listening to your gut and allowing it to guide your decisions. On the other hand, it's not about completely listening to hunches and ignoring logic and other signs, it's about using all of the tools available to you and allowing them to combine together to create a full armory of tools.

Trusting Your Inner Voice

The biggest problem with the concept of intuition is that most people don't trust it. The reason is that it can't be explained. As humans, we like things we can understand, things we can apply logic to and reason with. There is no way to put an actual scientific definition on intuition, it is simply something that is. You can't even argue that it's not there, because we all experience it, and we've all had situations where we've had feelings that we can't explain.

The fact there is no logic to back up intuition can mean that some people go through life never really trusting their gut. The sad thing about that fact is that their gut was trying to help them and had they taken a chance and listened to it, they could have made better decisions, seen things that they were subconsciously ignoring, and enriched their lives as a result. Of course, in some extreme cases, listening to their gut could have kept them safe, when the outcome was something completely different.

So, how can you learn to listen to your intuition? Building trust in your intuition is a little like building muscle at the gym; you need to flex those muscles in order to make them stronger, and the stronger they are, the more prevalent they become in your life. Consider your intuition as a muscle that you need to work out and dedicate the same amount of time and effort to it as you would lifting weights in the gym.

You first need to understand what your intuition feels like. Some people say it feels like a warm glow, others say it feels like a nagging sensation, and others say it feels like a weight in the pit of their stomach. How your intuition feels to you is a personal deal and you need to tune into it and learn how it feels, so you can identify it when it comes into your life. Remember, your intuition isn't there all the time, it simply crops up at times when it is needed, and you need to identify the feeling and not confuse it with something else, in order to start listening to it and trusting what it is telling you.

The other confusing part about intuition is that it isn't going to come to you in a verbal form. You're to going to experience a strange feeling, alerting you to the fact that your intuition is in full swing and then suddenly a voice from above tells you what you need to know! It is a feeling, something you just "know", and that's what most people struggle with. How do you actually know what it is that your intuition is telling you? That's where trust comes in and trusting your own judgment.

The single best way to learn how to trust your intuition is to blindly follow it and see where it leads you. Know that you will be safe and that nothing bad is going to happen and allow the flow to continue on. As your logic tries to reason with your own mind, push it away and explore the feeling, trying to identify the thoughts that pop into your mind.

For example, the following situation has nothing to do with analyzing a person, but it is a good example of how to understand what your intuition is trying to tell you in a visual form.

Imagine that you have been offered a job and you're not sure whether to take it or not. Sure, it has perks, possibly even better pay, but there is something stopping you from jumping for joy and saying "yes". That 'something' is your intuition. It might feel like a nagging doubt, in this case, something you can't quite put your finger on. When you feel that way, you need to stop and explore it.

Ask yourself what you feel uneasy about and try and visualize yourself in the job. What color springs to your mind first? Is it a bright, happy color? Or, is it a dark, forbidding color? Many people say that their intuition gives them information via visual images and via color. If the job looks dark to you in your vision, then your intuition is telling you that it's not quite right, for whatever reason. You might never get to know what that exact reason is, but you know it's not right, and it feels right when you say to yourself "I don't think this job is right for me". The feeling will change right at that moment. The nagging doubt will go, and you will suddenly feel like the choice is right not to take it.

On the other hand, if the job looks bright and in your vision, you are smiling, your intuition is guiding you towards it.

You can understand from that example why some people struggle with the idea of intuition, considering it to be some type of psychic ability, but it's not psychic at all. It's simply your brain and your subconscious trying to come together to help you make the right decision for you. If your intuition is nagging at you, it's because you already know something deep down, but you're simply pushing the thought away and not listening to it.

From that example, the next course of action would be to turn that job down. Your logic might be screaming at you, "but it's better to pay", but you know that you wouldn't be happy there, and the dark feel of the job when you explored it in detail, gave you that information.

It's also important to know that it's completely normal to have doubts when you first start following your intuition, and even after you begin to trust it completely. Our minds are hard-wired to be a little suspicious; it's the way we learn to survive and get through difficult situations. What you need to do is be sure that you have made the right choice to follow your gut, and simply allow the rest of the story to play out.

What you will probably notice is that by trusting your gut and following what it tells you, you never stray too far wrong. The more you do it, the more you will trust your intuition, and the easier it will become to go with your gut in the future.

Intuition And Analyzing Other People/Situations

In terms of analyzing other people, your intuition is vitally important. You might simply get a feeling that something just 'isn't right' about a person or situation, but you have no real evidence to back it up. Of course, you need evidence if you're going to accuse someone of doing something or saying something, but you should also listen to your gut in terms of whether you pursue the situation, or whether you leave it be.

Again, learning how to trust your gut and going with what it tells you, whether your brain is telling you you're crazy or not, is the only way to really understand what your gut is trying to tell you. If you avoid listening to it, you will always wonder if you were right or not.

The bottom line is that we tend to see what we want to see, and we push the things we don't want to believe away. This can certainly be the case with a person. Perhaps this is a person you are in love with and you have a nagging suspicion that they're cheating. Of course, it's not a good idea to jump straight in with the accusations, but you should listen to your intuition and allow it to guide you in trying to learn more. Your gut isn't trying to ruin your relationship or hurt you, it's trying to prevent you from going down a path that is going to ultimately lead you towards heartbreak and even more hurt than you will experience in finding out the truth in here and now.

So, when you get a hunch about a person or a situation, don't jump straight in and take action, use that hunch to allow you to explore further. Listen to what it is telling you and look for evidence. The chance is that you will find it by looking at someone's body language, listening to their words and how they say them, and pulling everything together. In this case, your intuition is guiding you, and that is what is it meant to do.

When you hear someone saying: "something just didn't add up", or "I had a strange feeling about him/her", that is them listening to their intuition about a person and allowing it to guide their analysis further. Through blindly trusting your hunches, you will be able to become far surer in your ability to understand what your gut is trying to tell you.

It's a lot to take in, that's for sure. Intuition is something which whilst it cannot be explained, is extremely real. Scientists had the idea of intuition and gut feelings because they can't measure them. There is no data to record, no case studies to examine with actual physical evidence, and simply a feeling that should be followed. That is why you will hear so much negativity from certain people about this very subject. The thing is, those people who talk negatively about intuition simply don't trust it and have never tried.

Surely, it's better to try and find out for yourself?

Separating Intuition From Paranoia

One of the biggest challenges you will face when you first start trying to listen to and trust your intuition is trying to decide whether you're just being a little paranoid, or whether you really are hearing your intuition trying to guide you. This can certainly be the case in certain situations, i.e. when you really don't want to believe something bad about a person, or you really don't want to believe that something is wrong with someone close to you. It's easy for the mind to play tricks, and when you don't trust your intuition, it can be all too easy to question it and pass it off as nonsense.

So, how can you get around this problem?

It's really about trusting yourself and you cannot get around the fact that you are going to question and doubt your intuition at the start; it's natural, it's part and parcel of learning to let go of logic to a certain degree, and allow your gut to guide you, bearing in mind other necessary information that comes your way.

Intuition and paranoia tend to feel different, but only subtly so. When you're so hard-wired to be negative it's easy to go with the paranoia route and forget that there might be another road, but if you want to analyze people effectively, you need to be prepared to cut the reins a little and just go with it.

Paranoia tends to feel negative, but intuition feels more like something you can't quite put your finger on. Intuition isn't telling you definitely one way or another regarding a person or a situation, it's telling you to delve a little deeper, it's telling you something isn't quite as it seems. In that respect, intuition may feel a little like suspicion. On the other hand, paranoia will feel definite and negative. By tuning into how you feel when you experience a situation, you're not sure is paranoia or intuition, you'll be able to learn how to tell the difference over time.

The best course of action is to go with it. You will never learn unless you take a few calculated risks. So, the next time you get that gut feeling, don't question it and don't assume it's your mind playing tricks, or that you're being paranoid. Instead, dare to explore the feeling a little more, allowing your faith to follow you into the sensation. How does it feel, can you visualize what you're feeling? Remember, we mentioned colors earlier on, and that is often a good way to tell whether something is positive or negative, in terms of the darkness or light shade of color pertaining to a situation.

Sometimes you might find yourself following a hunch which turns out to be wrong, but that's simply part and parcel of the deal. Your intuition is not going to be 100% right all the time, especially at the start. It's important however that you don't allow small setbacks to throw you off course and to allow yourself to become untrusting of what you're feeling. Give yourself time, and you will get there!

Of course, it could be that you felt the intuition and you went with it, but you decided on the wrong course of action. Again, this is quite likely and something you need to be prepared for. In that situation, it's not your intuition which was off, it's your decision making that was incorrect instead.

Learning to trust your intuition means throwing the idea of being paranoid out of the window. It's also about discarding the notion that you have to be right all the time. Sometimes you'll read a situation wrong, and that stands for those who have been analyzing others for years too. You read about police investigations that didn't yield results, and a few years down the line it might come to light that there was a clue there all along. Humans are not foolproof when it comes to reading situations and making the right choices. Sometimes we get it wrong, but when you follow your intuition, most of the time you will get it right.

How to Use Intuition Alongside Logic

One of the best ways to increase your success rate is to allow logic and intuition to coexist side by side. You might wonder how that is even possible because surely one would play off the other and cause confusion and even paranoia? Not always, but certainly at the start that could be an issue.

When you get a hunch, when something feels a little off, or a little voice on your shoulder is telling you to delve a little deeper, acknowledge that feeling and signal your intention to do exactly what your hunch is telling you to do - examine the situation deeper. From that, your logic and the skills you've learned so far, about body language and verbal cues, will take over.

As you can see, intuition isn't about solving the riddle from start to finish, it's a gentle nudge in the direction to do so. Once you have received the message from your intuition, it's time for logic to become the guide. They both work hand in hand, and it's about allowing them both to sit together, and not favoring one over the other.

When you first start getting results from listening to your intuition, it's easy to focus entirely on that and not listen to any other line of inquiry. The problem is, if you do that, you're likely to miss something important.

Consider this - if a police inquiry focused entirely on body language and hunches, would the investigation ever get solved? No, because things need tomato sense, and that is where logic comes into it. Yes, hunches should be listened to, and yes, if you get a feeling about something you should explore it further, but you also have to apply logic in order to close the situation and come to a conclusion.

You cannot say to someone "I believe you're lying because I just sense it". They're going to laugh at you and ask what proof you have. You have none. You might feel you're right, in fact, you probably are, but you need to produce proof in order to back up your claims otherwise they're going to fall on deaf ears.

The bottom line is that proof is always out there, you just need to know when to look for it; your intuition is the guide that will tell you to do that, and when you allow both sides of the coin to work harmoniously together, you'll notice a bigger success rate than if you lean simply on logic or intuition alone.

Combining Body Language and Verbal Cues

With all this talk of listening to your gut and going with your hunches, how do you apply logic? We've just mentioned that you need to use both your brain and your gut if you want to make decisions and analyze people effectively and accurately. Part of that is combining body language cues and verbal cues and allowing the blend of the two to bring you to a conclusion.

There are so many different combinations we could talk about here, and we would be here all day. For instance, a few of the most common body language and verbal cues are:

- Refusing to make eye contact and stumbling over words can mean they're lying

- Holding fleeting eye contact, seeming distracted, speaking in a low voice, whilst also struggling to find words, with 'um' and 'ah' mentioned a lot, can mean that they are distracted by an issue or struggling with something

- Holding your eye contact in quite an aggressive way whilst crossing their arms across their body in a defensive stance, turning questions onto you rather than answering your questions can mean that they are hiding something and also lying about it

As you can see, combinations can mean different things. Someone who refuses to hold your eye contact doesn't necessarily have to be lying, it completely depends upon the other signs you pick up on which work alongside it.

The key is to piece together the information you have and to avoid jumping to conclusions before you have analyzed everything as one. One piece of evidence alone can mean one thing, but when you combine it with one or more additional pieces of evidence, the story could change, and you are led to a completely different conclusion.

It will certainly take you a lot longer to analyze people and situations at the start, but you will become quicker and more accurate as you gain experience. It might also be that you stumble a few times at the start and perhaps get it wrong, but don't let that stop you from continuing to try and analyze other people when the situation calls for it.

What is Personal Perception?

Are intuition and personal perception the same thing? No. One leads to the other, and in this case, your intuition leads you to personal perception.

Personal perception is how you read a situation. Everyone will read a situation slightly differently, hence the 'personal' part of the phrase. Your intuition will lead you to analyze a situation, and from there you will also take into account body language and verbal cues, as well as any behavioral points you can see. Your personal perception is then what you decide the situation is, e.g. the conclusion you reach.

The interesting this is that you can read a situation and use your perception to arrive at your own personal decision, but someone else can read the same situation and perhaps come to a slightly different conclusion. We all read things differently, take things in different ways, and we're all slightly more sensitive to certain subjects than others. This is what makes analyzing people accurately quite difficult - everyone may perceive something to be different!

For instance, a shy person may come across as ignorant to one person, but another person might instantly be able to read that they're shy. One person might instantly click with them, whilst another may simply assume, they're rude and want nothing to do with them. How we perceive situations and people can vary slightly, but it's never too far from the mark from person to person.

There is nothing you can do about your own personal perception because it is a natural setting you have within yourself. What you can do is learn to be more accurate, by ensuring that you take everything into account, and not just jumping to conclusions which may be slightly wide of the mark. You could argue that this is why police inquiries have to be backed up by evidence. Not only because evidence ensures fairness of justice, but also because the way one office may perceive a situation may be slightly different from the way another office perceives a situation. It's a personal setting, and not always reflective of truth or reality. What it can do however is lead you towards the truth, provided you keep an open mind.

Key Points From This Chapter

Learning to listen to your intuition is one thing but learning to trust it is quite another. Before you even get to that point, it's important to understand what it actually feels like to experience your intuition kicking into action.

This will be different for everyone, but a feeling of something being not quite right, or a hunch to dig deeper is usually how it feels. Some people report their intuition as feeling a little like butterflies, whilst others say they can't quite put their finger on what to call it, it's simply a hunch, a subtle push, and a nagging doubt. What you do need do is identify what intuition feels like for you and then explore it a little more. The only way to trust your intuition is to follow it blindly and see where it takes you. Yes, that is a risk to a certain degree, but your intuition is never going to lead you into danger; it's actually there to keep you safe!

Identifying the difference between intuition and paranoia is also important, but there is no easy route towards achieving this. Again, it comes down to blind trust and going with what you feel. Paranoia and intuition feel subtly different, with paranoia tending to have a negative, darker feeling, compared the nudging feeling of intuition. Again, this will be different for everyone.

We've covered a lot of information in this chapter, and there are no easy answers to how you can learn to trust that gut feeling and be confident that it is leading you in the right direction. All you can do is just go with it and see where you end up!

The key points to take from this chapter are:

- Your intuition is there to guide you away from danger and to give you gentle pushes towards situations which may benefit you
- Intuition and paranoia are two very different things, but they can easily be confused
- Learning to trust your intuition is difficult because it takes blind faith. The only way to be able to confidently rely upon your intuition is to go with it
- Intuition alone cannot be relied upon to analyze other people; you need to use your intuition to lead you towards situations and to tell

you when something isn't quite right, and then use body language and verbal cues to form a full picture

- Body language and verbal cues should be used together in order analyze a person, and whilst it might take time at first to form an overall conclusion, this will become easier and faster, the more you practice analyzing other people

- Personal perception is the final conclusion you arrive at, e.g. the way you perceive a situation

- Intuition comes before personal perception. Intuition is the hunch that something isn't quite right, and perception is the final result in terms of your analysis.

Conclusion

We're now at the end of our journey into the art of analyzing people, and by now you should be feeling brimming full of ideas and confidence, ready to practice your own skills.

The art of analyzing other people takes time, that's a certainty, and you shouldn't be disheartened if you struggle with accuracy or piecing things together at first. If analyzing people was easy, we would all be doing it from birth, and there would be no hope for anyone who was lying or hiding anything!

Being able to analyze other people isn't always for negative reasons. Yes, there are many unscrupulous people out there, and a lot of people who will lie, cheat and try to deceive, but that doesn't mean that is everyone's agenda. Being able to accurately analyze people can also be used for positive reasons. Perhaps you have a friend who is hiding a problem, not speaking to anyone about it and therefore trying to cope on their own. Nobody should have to do that, and by you listening to your intuition and using the information to analyze them, you can identify the issue and ask them if they want to talk. This could be all it takes to help take a load off their shoulders, and for you to be able to help them with whatever their problem is.

Of course, being able to analyze someone can also save you from deception and manipulation, but it's important to know when to use your skills and then to let things be. Not every situation requires analysis, and sometimes you just need to let things go and see where life takes you. The ability to be able to use analysis in specific moments, however, is something you will rely upon time and time again through your life.

Does it happen overnight? No. Will you always get it right? Certainly not. What you can rely on is that as you use your skills more and more, and as you become more confident, learning to trust your intuition rather than doubting it, you'll notice that your accuracy improves, and you'll notice that you feel more confident and sure in what you're doing. Learning to analyze people is the same as any other skill - you need to practice and understand that time is all that is required.

Anyone can learn these skills, you don't need to have any specific background or under-standing, you simply need an open mind and the ability to be able to pick up on signals and trust them. Perhaps trusting the ideas you're coming up with is the hardest part of them all. Most of us are naturally untrusting, either of other people or in regard to ourselves, and that is why so many people don't actually know how to use their own natural intuition.

Learning to analyze other people is made up of three main sections, and within those sections, there are subcategories too. These are:

• Understanding body language

• Understanding verbal language

• Trusting your intuition

Within body language, you need to be able to know which signals usually relate to which emotion or situation and use those in conjunction with the verbal language cues. Within that section you have gone, the language selected speed of speech and other behavioral aspects. Finally, you have intuition. Intuition can either be the starting point of your analysis or the endpoint, it really depends upon the situation.

For instance, you might notice negative body language and then start picking up on language cues. From there, you might start to piece it all together, but you have a hunch from your intuition telling you to go in a specific direction. It could also work the other way; perhaps you just have a hunch from the start, and that leads you to start analyzing body language and speech. Your intuition is very flexible, but it's a skill and an asset which most people either ignore or don't allow to flourish.

You might have read through the book and still be doubting your analysis skills, but again, this comes down to confidence. Trust in yourself and allow yourself to follow whatever hunches come your way. You certainly don't have to analyze every situation and issue you stumble across, but you should certainly follow the ones which simply have a spark of intuition attached to them. If you suspect someone is struggling with a problem but not opening up, follow it, and if you suspect that someone truly is lying, follow that too. What you shouldn't do is go around accusing everyone you suspect to be lying of actually doing that! Some people can disguise their real feelings and problems and mask them in different was. For instance, someone who is shy may easily come across as cold or as though they are acting in a suspicious way - it doesn't mean that they are!

Put simply, you will get yourself into trouble if you accuse others without having actual evidence but by analyzing their behavior, you'll probably glean enough to be sure within yourself. In most cases, that's all you need; you don't necessarily have to call everyone out.

Key Points From This Book

We can't possibly highlight every single point of importance from the book, but we can pull out some of the main points for you to remember and read back over. Remember, if ever you doubt yourself or you're struggling to remember what to do, you always have this book to recap on and help you regain your confidence.

The main points to take away from this book are:

- The ability to analyze other people isn't a gift, it is something which can be learned and practiced by anyone
- There are many situations in which being able to analyze another person will be useful to you, including being able to help someone who is struggling to open up, to catching someone out who you suspect to be lying to you
- It's important to be thorough in your analysis and does not accuse anyone of something you're not sure of

- There are three main facets to analyzing a person - body language, verbal cues, and using your own intuition

- The police often read body language cues to help them decide whether or not someone is lying or hiding something, but this is always backed up by solid evidence. Body language is a pointer in the right direction, not a hard and fast reason for an arrest!

- Body language can either be negative or positive, and it's rarely wrong

- A person is able to mask their body language to a certain degree, but only in a situation which they know is coming up, e.g. if they're trying to appear less nervous during a job interview. They can do this by being aware of positive and negative body language signals and consciously trying to cut down on the negative and push more towards the positive

- Verbal cues can often be disguised, i.e. with lies, but when reading in conjunction with body language, it's possible to understand the truth of the situation

- Verbal language includes the words chosen, the speed of the words being spoken, and tone of voice. You can only analyze the verbal accurately when you put together all of these elements

- Behavioral tactics will also help you understand what is going on, but you need to be able to understand these, as they can often fly beneath the radar. The most common are turning a situation around on you, turning everything into a question, accusing you of doing what you're suggesting they're doing, gas lighting, and distraction techniques

- The speed someone speaks to you at is often more telling than the words they use. Someone who is lying, hiding something, or nervous, will speak quickly

- Personal perception and intuition are linked, i.e. intuition is a hunch, whilst the perception is what you read and take that hunch to mean when used in conjunction with body language and verbal cues

- It is important to keep an open mind, despite what you might be formulating in your mind - you won't get it right all the time

- Learning to trust your intuition, in order to allow it to guide you in life, is a process which takes a lot of practice and most of the time it is about blinding following it and seeing where it leads you

- Paranoia and intuition feel very different, but knowing the difference also takes practice

- Paranoia often feels dark and negative, whereas intuition usually has no solid words to describe it, i.e. a hunch, or simply push towards a specific direction or line of inquiry

That is a brief summary of the points to re-member, but that is only part of the story! Remember to read back through the book whenever you need guidance, or your intuition or perception is waving a little.

A Final Word About Intuition

Before we bid you goodbye and allow you to run wild with practicing your new analysis skills, let's give you one last word about intuition.

Learning to trust your gut will help you in so many different situations throughout your life, not only in terms of analyzing other people. It's important that you allow yourself the time and space to develop these skills if you want to really ensure accuracy.

Aside from that, intuition is there to keep you safe in all situations and it's also there to push you towards helping others. You've no doubt experienced a hunch in your life before, but perhaps you never acted on it. If you had acted on it, you would probably have discovered something either new, interesting, or perhaps an opportunity you might like to have explored more.

Intuition cannot be explained and that's what makes it so confusing for many. The fact that we can't logically explain something often means we don't believe it, but that is a mistake. You can't see oxygen, but you trust that it's there! Of course, you can measure oxygen, and perhaps that is the difference between why we believe something that is invisible versus our intuition.

You will never be able to put the measurement of proof on your intuition, but you should certainly trust it regardless.

All that's left to do is to bid you goodbye. Trust yourself, build your confidence and allow your skills to build. Not only will you avoid difficult situations in your own life, but you might also be able to help others, who may be finding it hard to open up and ask for help verbally.

Read back over anything you don't understand, but above all else, listen to and trust your intuition at all times.

59511750R00068

Made in the USA
Middletown, DE
12 August 2019